Paradise Notes

Poems by Patricia Traxler

Spartan
Press

Spartan Press

Kansas City, Missouri

spartanpresskc.com

Spartan
Press

Author photo: Patrick Wallerius

Cover image: Jan Brueghel (the Elder),

care of the Carmen Thyssen Collection

Acknowledgments:

In the decades since Patricia Traxler moved to Salina from San Diego, she has been active in the cultural life of the city and she taught at Kansas Wesleyan University for more then three decades. Traxler is the author of four previous volumes of poetry, including most recently *Naming the Fires*, a novel, *Blood*, and a short-story collection, *In the Skin*. She is working on a collection of essays, *Don't Ask Me*, and a volume of her collected poems, as yet untitled. *Paradise Notes* is her fifth poetry collection.

TABLE OF CONTENTS

for Eric and Angela,
and in memory of Christian

But we must lose our earthly Paradise
in order actually to live in it, to
experience it in the reality of its
images in the absolute sublimation
that transcends all passion.

-Gaston Bachelard, *The Poetics of Space*

Paradise Notes

INNOCENCE

The simplest things I've loved inspire wonder in me
now, or wound me—morning glories crawling over
the splintered fence at first light on Wightman Street;
seaweed nudging me beneath the mossy sway of salt
waves while my parents spread towels over the sand;
my mother's long-ago garden and her eternal certainty;
my Irish grandmother's room astir with handwritten
poems that burnt through the page; my father's hands
and knees so stained from work they wouldn't clean;
my older brother bent over his study of the Phaestos
Disc as he ate alone in his room while the other ten of
us gathered at the table—and all around me there the
chatter of six younger siblings whose diapers I'd once
changed, and whose mouths had opened eagerly for
soft meals I'd spoon from Gerber's jars. We were all
together there, once, in our small house, sharing meals
our mother prepared with supplies we bought from
Benny Yee, the neighborhood grocer who allowed us to
charge our weekly purchases on a store account because
we had to eat, and he trusted we would always pay

eventually. Would I bring it all back tonight if I could, because it was true? Is childhood ever our own truth, anyway? Don't I prefer the comfort, now, of quiet and solitary nights with my own thoughts and music and my self-directed labor to occupy me? I wonder if memory misnames itself as happiness, and if anyone was truly happy in our old days. Or did we withhold our discontent from one another in order to keep our life together? Didn't we leave it all the very moment we found a way?

THE UNKNOWING

Yes, I remember how it felt to be alive
with a longing that scalded flesh and mind
as nothing would again, or could, after.

I have myself to blame, that I know. The rest
no longer matters. I can live with it, and will
if I'm to live the life I must. Yes, I was untried,

but I was not a child. In fact, I was no longer
even young. Simply alone. I've come to realize
that was your key. Now, where are the words

That were born in me? I want them back. I'll speak
with my own mouth, find my way through this
dark to an arc of light, a different knowing.

Before all else must come the telling, after all
the years, though you wouldn't want me to,
wouldn't want your unknowables known.

It was simple, brilliant, how you opened me, swore me
to secrecy, then told the world the things you'd said I
mustn't tell. You held me close for years, decades,

Moving through my world and out again and in, and yes,
I welcomed you, always. You were illumination, a burning
word, dance of irresistable power. The hunger grew in me,

The light of your knowing seared me, flesh and mind, spirit
and bone. That wanting, yes, I felt it with every step, every word,
breath and gesture illuminated by the thought of you, indelible,

Undeniable, true. And realizing you needed no one
to know, I spoke only to a trusted stillness. You spoke
to your most trusted dozen friends, and they told the world

For you. And then they knew, all of them, or thought they knew.
Did they see me an object of desire or, more likely, of pity or derision?
I kept truth and excuses recorded and stored in a foreign tongue.

And then I found you'd gone without a word, and as the truth
announced itself, days became nattering ghosts of memory.
Nights, I would wake to the astonishment of your absence.

Occasionally I'd see you out somewhere, brandishing yourself
before the world like a sword just pulled from a sacred stone.
I remained at a distance, having left the world where curious eyes

Clung to my skin. Even now I can feel their gaze, those eyes,
wanting to know--not about me, but you. Soiled flesh was what
I felt they saw of me, and I found myself guilty of believing

That image to be true. You went on to much applause. I chose
to remain in the quiet I knew and stayed there years, without
certainty of what I was awaiting. You called, wrote, persisted.

I locked myself when you left, and from time to time
you returned unannounced, your eyes shining through
the resolute dark, where your touch woke and silenced me.

Time, generous taker, delicate brute. Years. Decades.
Always the voice in my ear, drowning sounds of the world.
Once, I lived in your dream, let it fill me. Yes, I died

Several times but, unable to sustain it, I slept in a cocoon
of my own making, time disguising itself as life, until I woke
to the knowing or it woke me, all those secrets abloom in the dark.

I no longer wish to see the world you see, to know what you
desire, what you're able to feel. Leave me, finally, whoever you
really are. The sky is quiet, the air is still. Leave me now. I'm home.

EVERYTHING

You don't want me
to know, but I know:
You don't own the world
anymore. Yes, I remember
your touch, I'll admit; but if
you stood here now,
beside me at the edge
of this field that has just
set wheat again, my eyes
would be fixed on what has grown
green and new before me
and beyond you and I might
not remember how it felt to know
you when our world was here,
when you were everything.

GILEAD

There is no reason to speak here.
There's no one to listen. Indifference
is mistaken for calm, and a word will
often endure beyond its own meaning.
Take care what thoughts you speak,
what ideas you allow to invade your ear.
This is the way it was before the storm
that took everything away and allowed
the mute to speak again as if, even then,
there could be anything to say.

LULLABY FOR THE DAY

The day is coming again, I note its return
each year, the day that holds the hour
when my body opened to give the earth
my son. It has him, holds him hard beneath
a stone with no last name engraved, his body
long since one with dark adobe soil overlaid
with wild milkweed, crabgrass, fallen
eucalyptus leaves, yellowing pine needles.

There is a man I do not know who tends the
baby graves, who has a book with all the names
inside. I wonder, does he sometimes think he hears
the lost ones calling as he treads the rows? Did
my son feel me there the day I found the spot
where they'd planted him while I still lay in the
birthing bed? The doctors let his father see him
but slid a needle full of sleep into me without warning,
to make me sleep, sleep away his first and only
living hours of a single day; then someone put him
in the ground, it seems, so I'd forget him.

I found him where they'd left him and I knelt there
pulling crabgrass from his grave, stuffing it into my pocket
like a thief, grave-robber, and I took it home with me.
I keep it in a small cloth bag that can cover the palm
of an open hand like salve over a wound. Time tells
the world nothing at all, only forces its mute years
between us while that first light dims and loses its sway;
It doesn't matter, doesn't matter because even in the
consecrated silence I move closer, closer to him every day.

THE DEER

In darkness beside the empty road he must have
waited and then, drawn by the approaching light,
in a microsecond he's leapt from the shelter
of cottonwoods into the swath of my beams. I hear
and feel the impact, see him in profile arcing
upward, illuminated, hooves antlers hooves he
tumbles, amber eye opened wide and fixed on this
moment, his own sense of the world we share.

Stopping my crumpled car on the verge beside
a stand of cottonwood, oak, and blood-red sumac,
I see him in a heap across the road, look away,
make myself look back again. Then a slash of light,
truck pulling in behind my car. Someone wanting to
help, maybe. The man comes to my window, waves
a hand at the carcass, two of his fingers missing.

Are you going to eat the deer? he asks. By killing
a living creature, have I made it my own to give? I shake
my head, but then behind the man I see the deer lifting
his head and in a long moment, struggling to his feet
while the man waits for my answer. The deer staggers,

then bounds into the woods beyond the road. The man notes my gaze and turns. *Goddammit*, he says. *Fuck*.

Without another word he lopes back to his truck. His headlights come on again, illuminating my car's interior. my hands still on the wheel. I watch him take the road, disappear. The wind returns and cottonwoods stir. What

other life might be waiting, hidden beneath rough boughs in darkness? The engine hesitates, then catches. Enclosed in buckled metal, I move back onto the road, watching shadows and shapes along the edge for signs of life.

THE CERULEAN ROOM

I dreamed I was painting my mother's
last room for my older brother
and me to live in, and as I worked I
imagined him living on one side
of the room, and me on the other, our
shared memories aloft in the air
like fireflies, creating their own light.

In the dream there's a curtain strung across
the room between us because we're likely to
argue otherwise--and anyway, neither of us ever
liked a crowd. Plus, he's a nudist. We both favor
books, music, our own thoughts, maybe a cat or
dog nearby, a blank notebook to fill with words
or images, and an ocean within our hearing.

I was painting our mother's last room for the two
of us to live in, all of our memories alive there
in the blue air. Our mother is dead. So is our father.
My brother lives in Uruguay, where he spends his
days and nights translating 14th century Kashmiri
poetry. I haven't seen his face in years. I was

painting the walls of the room cerulean blue
like the sky, like heaven, like an imagined eternity,
and I was humming as I covered more and more
of the room in blue. As I worked, a fine peace settled
into my head and my heart and our memories became
a choir of some sort in the air of the room, our home;
I couldn't see my brother and he couldn't see me, but
each of us knew the other was there, and I just went on
painting, painting, painting, as if our world could never end.

THE LOST

The lost ones sing in the sea, their mouths opening
to saltwater, brine, and bone. They sleep in shifting
shadows there, beneath whatever is or was or could
have been. A confusion of mother-tongues tangle
in the waves and, rising singly, evaporate in air.

Sometimes you hear them calling you to land's edge,
and you follow the sound to its end, lie down in the low
lapping tide where your body is blessedly nothing, its
outline just the beginning of everything else. You may ask,
Why did you leave so soon? Or, *Why were you never here?*

The sky goes black as you enter the restless water
like a lover, moving forward beneath it, half-blind,
measuring distances with your limbs, the weight of the
sea pressing in. Soon you've forgotten when you last
breathed air, last felt anything at all beyond the tremble

a far-off promise will send through deepest sea. Your
hands spread like fans in the water, and you swim as you never
could in daylight, measuring the enormity against your body.
The ocean pulls you down, and night lowers itself to meet you,

filling the water. When you look up, you no longer see light
riding the surface. Your mouth opens, and the names of the lost
become saltwater in your throat. You swallow willingly, sinking
deeper into water that now springs clear and pure. This is the world
you dreamed of, far from the burning stars, far from life as you've
known it, and for a moment before you rise into the world
of light, you can wash your hands among the innocent again.

LETTER TO A DREAM

America, how can I hear you above the din?
How could you leave me after all we've been
through together? Often, in the fresh news of a
damp dawn I've tried to find you again, and again
in the soft, bruised skies of evening I've looked
for you. Once, you were everywhere, like God.
I could feel. you wherever I went. You were
the old woman in black who walked our street
with a bag to collect whatever she found, you were
the broken soldiers on the bus when I rode home
from school each afternoon, you were the loud TV
and the smell of dinner in our house, babies crying
or cooing, the phone ringing. Mrs. Cornell next door
calling her grandkids in to see their mom who was
visiting from her new life. You were small, random
airplanes high in the unmuddled sky, their engines
emitting a soft, plaintive cry. Lately, it seems I don't
know you anymore, nor am I even certain who you
ever were. I thnk maybe you seemed better when
I was a child, easier to comprehend as our small,
shabby block of Wightman Street where I knew
everyone, where I could smell their suppers cooking
in the evening, those meals wafting and mixing,
blessing the air with a promise impossible to keep.

WATCHING THE CREDITS ROLL

The movie had just ended and I didn't want to wait for the credits to finish rolling before I got up from my seat because these days you can find that stuff on the internet when you get home anyway so I headed down the stairs from my seat in the dark while the credits rolled and I missed a step and fell I hurtled forward into the dark and as I sailed thru the air the world changed and changed, people were born and died, Donald Trump was impeached, and my lost child was found. Music was written and recorded and played and forgotten and became oldies and was forgotten again, my next book wrote itself, sold modestly, and was remaindered. I developed a sense of direction and learned to swim. My parents returned from the dead with their dead baby whom I'd never met. The man I loved enough to remake a world for died, and died, he died and now I know that I will never know that feeling again but I am free, free of love and free of the god who may or may not exist but who allowed me to lose my son, and my love and thus freed from the rigors and strictures of feeling and belief I flew through the air and landed on the multicolored midcentury style carpet just as the credits finished rolling and a new war was beginning somewhere in the Middle East and everyone I'd lost was lost again, and it was peaceful there on the midcentury carpet, I could see a piece of popcorn near my face on the floor so I reached for it and popped it into my mouth and someone asked me if they could help me up, ma'am, and I said please don't call me ma'am just go about your business as if I weren't even here because I'm waiting waiting waiting for my son to come back, waiting for life as I know it to end, waiting to know the secret at the center of things, the word that must be spoken at the gate, waiting for the reason to live, I must have missed it on the way down, waiting for love to be equal and free and fair, waiting for skin color not to matter, for freedom to be free, waiting for life to say yes to all who want it and let the small crowd that has gathered around me go home and let me be, because I kind of like it here, I enjoy the press of my cheek on the multicolored midcentury carpet, I swallow the kernel of popcorn I found, close my eyes and wait for the movie to begin again.

OCTOBER GRACKLES

Hundreds of you, everywhere above me,
lining every branch of every tree,
you own the day. I can't love you.
Go, leave my elms and oaks, ash
and cottonwood, continue on your way,
sharp voices etching pure October air.

You need only yourselves, your song
and propaganda. I understand this.
Once, I was like you, craving change and stir,
the momentary fancy. And then I was here,
where place became time. Now, give me back
the stillness, please, and I will give you this:
Hurry, leave, before you lose the will to fly.

ELEGY FOR A BROKEN WORLD

Wherever we go, things look the same as always:
Along the Pacific coast, the ancient Torrey pines stand
in place on cliffs high above the ocean, twisted and bent
like aging dancers stilled by time's deliberation.

In the heartland, where there was always evangelical suspicion,
winter wheat survives fierce springtime storms, but neighbors
suspect neighbors of voting to destroy sacred traditions, and in
quiet rural enclaves people pray together above basements
crammed with rations and stacked with automatic weapons.

Shore to shore, our great cities continue to buzz and jump
and shout and buy and clamor. The underground trains depart
without incident; art and theatre thrive. And yet, across the land
our light has dimmed, and we find our certitude diminishing.

Still, we try to trust our world, unmoored, untended, wasting
at its core, we try to love it, whoever leads it, even as wild
threats and harsh pronouncements weight the air. Everywhere
we turn, long-buried words emerge--angry, unsorted, of malleable
truth and uncertain provenance--to become our lingua franca.

Freedom's a concept we once lived with easily, as if we had
invented it. In fact, I guess we thought we had. Autumn returns
now, in all its rehearsed glory, as if it had a right, as if the world
were still our own--but now the news is never new, although

We will watch and read and listen while autumn winds send
bright, dry leaves skittering across the land again, past scars we
feel but cannot see. We try to love our broken world, try to summon
words of praise for what remains of it, alive and good in us, and we lie
to help ourselves believe it can be returned to us in time for saving.

AFTER

Oh, we become so maudlin at the edge
of eternity, as if no one else has been
here, or will be. Where are the trumpets,
the swans, the assembled masses?
The quiet air rebukes us. See there,
the stray orange tom creeping by like a felon,
belly close to the stones. He's past his prime
but still on the hunt. Nearby, the blighted elm

Manages to acknowledge the seasons--and
what choice has it, rooted there? After years
of rehearsals, inarticulate goodbyes, after everything,
what's left to us but the stern economy of days
and the sound of our own footfall in the hollow
of night--you, alone there, hesitant, new as a child.

Patricia Traxler is the author of five poetry collections, including the 2019 Kansas Book Award winner, *Naming the Fires,* and of a novel, *Blood,* and a short story collection, *In the Skin.* She has twice been named Bunting Poetry Fellow at Radcliffe, and has read or served as resident poet at many other universities, including Ohio State, Harvard University, Kansas University, the University of Montana, and Utah State. Her work has appeared widely in print, including in *The Nation, The Boston Review, Agni, Ploughshares, Ms. Magazine, New Letters, The Los Angeles Times Literary Supplement, Slate,* and in the anthology *Best American Poetry.* Her novel, *Blood* (St. Martin's Minotaur), was also published in Spanish, German, and Swedish translations and in an Ireland/UK edition. This is her fifth poetry collection.

This project was made possible, in part, by generous support from the Osage Arts Community.

Osage Arts Community provides temporary time, space and support for the creation of new artistic works in a retreat format, serving creative people of all kinds — visual artists, composers, poets, fiction and nonfiction writers. Located on a 152-acre farm in an isolated rural mountainside setting in Central Missouri and bordered by ¾ of a mile of the Gasconade River, OAC provides residencies to those working alone, as well as welcoming collaborative teams, offering living space and workspace in a country environment to emerging and mid-career artists. For more information, visit us at www.osageac.org

Osage Arts Community

www.ingramcontent.com/pod-product-compliance
Lightning Source LLC
Chambersburg PA
CBHW031300120626
46545CB00007B/2914